Pebble
Plus

Countries

Egypt

by Christine Juarez

Consulting Editor: Gail Saunders-Smith, PhD

Pebble Plus is published by Capstone Press,
1710 Roe Crest Drive, North Mankato, Minnesota 56003
www.capstonepub.com

Library of Congress Cataloging-in-Publication Data
Juarez, Christine, 1976–
  Egypt / by Christine Juarez.
    pages cm.—(Pebble plus. Countries)
  Summary: "Simple text and full-color photographs illustrate the land, animals, and people of Egypt"—Provided by
publisher.
  Includes bibliographical references and index.
  ISBN 978-1-4765-4226-3 (library binding)—ISBN 978-1-4765-6041-0 (ebook PDF)
1. Egypt—Juvenile literature. I. Title.
  DT49.J83 2014
  962—dc23

5547   9223   01/15

2013031474

Editorial Credits
Erika L. Shores, editor; Bobbie Nuytten, designer; Tracy Cummins, media researcher; Laura Manthe, production specialist

Photo Credits
Alamy: Simon Reddy, 13; Newscom: David Rogers Africapictures.net, 11, MOHAMED OMAR/EPA, 14, Oliviero Olivieri/
Robert Harding, 17; Shutterstock: Baloncici, 19, Enrico Montanari, 7, Ivsanmas, 4, Mikael Damkier, 5, mrHanson, 9,
Ohmega1982, back cover (globe), RYGER, cover, 1 (design element), sculpies, 1, Vladimir Wrangel, 22 (flag), Winiki, 22
(currency), WitR, cover, 21

Note to Parents and Teachers

The Countries set supports national social studies standards related to people, places, and culture.
This book describes and illustrates Egypt. The images support early readers in understanding the
text. The repetition of words and phrases helps early readers learn new words. This book also
introduces early readers to subject-specific vocabulary words, which are defined in the Glossary
section. Early readers may need assistance to read some words and to use the Table of Contents,
Glossary, Read More, Internet Sites, and Index sections of the book.

Printed in the United States of America in North Mankato, Minnesota.
092013   007775CGS14

Table of Contents

Where Is Egypt?

Egypt is a country in northeast Africa. It is about three times the size of the U.S. state of New Mexico. Egypt's capital city is Cairo.

Cairo★

EGYPT

Landforms

Deserts are Egypt's main landforms.

The Western Desert is part

of the huge Sahara Desert.

The Arabian Desert lies

in eastern Egypt.

Animals

Egypt's wild animals live along the Nile River or in deserts. Snakes and lizards hide under rocks. Birds such as herons, storks, and cranes eat fish from the Nile.

heron

Language and Population

More than 85 million people live in Egypt. A little more than half the population lives in crowded cities. The other half lives in rural areas. Egyptians speak Arabic.

Food

Meals including bread and beans are common in Egypt. Egyptians eat stewed fava beans almost every day. They call this dish *fuul*.

Celebrations

Most Egyptians are Muslims
who follow the Islamic religion.
Muslims celebrate Eid al-Fitr
to mark the end of Ramadan.
Ramadan is a time of fasting.

15

Where People Work

Half of Egypt's people work service jobs. These jobs include teaching, banking, and selling. Outside the cities, most people farm. Farmers grow cotton, rice, and corn.

Transportation

Egyptians have many ways
to travel. Highways and railroads
join cities. People ride buses, trains,
cars, and bikes. Donkeys and
camels are used outside cities.

Famous Sight

Egyptians built huge pyramids more than 4,500 years ago. They buried Egyptian kings inside them. The largest pyramid is about 450 feet (137 meters) tall.

Country Facts

Name: Egypt

Capital: Cairo

Population: 85,294,388 (July 2013 estimate)

Size: 386,662 square miles (1,001,450 square kilometers)

Language: Arabic

Main Crops: cotton, rice, corn, beans, fruits

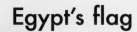

Egypt's flag

Money: Egyptian pound

Critical Thinking Using the Common Core

1. Look at the heron on page 9. Think about the bird's body. What makes the shores of the Nile River a good home for this bird? (Craft and Structure)

2. Rural desert areas have few roads. For what other reasons are camels good transportation in deserts? (Integration of Knowledge and Ideas)

Glossary

capital—the city in a country where the government is based

celebrate—to do something fun on a special day

crane—a large wading bird with long legs and a long neck and bill

desert—a dry area with little rain

fava bean—the large, flattened seed of a fava plant

heron—a bird with a long, thin beak and long legs

landform—a natural feature of the land

language—the way people speak or talk

Muslim—a person who follows the religion of Islam; Islam is based on the teachings of Muhammad

population—a group of people living in the same place

pyramid—a large Egyptian stone structure used as a place to bury kings

Ramadan—an Islamic religious holiday when Muslims fast

rural—having to do with the countryside

stork—a large bird with long, thin legs and a thin neck; storks wade in water

Read More

Kalman, Bobbie. *Spotlight on Egypt*. Spotlight on My Country. New York: Crabtree Pub., 2011.

Olson, Nathan. *Egypt in Colors*. World of Colors. Mankato, Minn.: Capstone Press, 2009.

Simmons, Walter. *Egypt*. Exploring Countries. Minneapolis: Bellwether Media, 2011.

Internet Sites

FactHound offers a safe, fun way to find Internet sites related to this book. All of the sites on FactHound have been researched by our staff.

Here's all you do:
Visit *www.facthound.com*
Type in this code: 9781476542263

Super-cool stuff!

Check out projects, games and lots more at
www.capstonekids.com

Index

Word Count: 229   Grade: 1   Early-Intervention Level: 20